The Unofficial Masterbuilt Smoker Cookbook

Complete Smoker Cookbook for Real Pitmasters, The Ultimate Guide for Smoking Meat, Fish, Game and Vegetables

DANIEL MURRAY

Table of Contents

AN INTRODUCTION TO SMOKED FOOD 6

CHAPTER 1: BEEF RECIPES 7

- MESMERIZING KOREAN BEEF RIBS 7
- INDIAN GROUND BEEF KEBABS 9
- ORIGINAL SOUTHERN BARBACOA 11
- TEXAS SMOKED BEEF BRISKET 13
- BBQ SMOKED CHUCK 15
- GENEROUSLY SMOKED BEEF STEW 17

CHAPTER 2: PORK RECIPES 19

- THE GREAT ANDOUILLE SAUSAGE 19
- PERFECTLY SMOKE APPLE BBQ PORK BELLY 21
- HICKORY PORK LOIN 23
- THE TRADITIONAL "NO FUSS" PORK SMOKE 25
- ALL-TIME FAVORITE PORK JERKY 27
- SUPER SPICY PORK LOIN WITH APPLE CABBAGE SLAW 29

CHAPTER 3: FISH AND SEAFOOD RECIPES 32

- SALMON AND VODKA DELIGHT 32
- LOVELY SMOKED SHRIMP 34
- GENTLE SMOKED TROUT 36
- PACIFIC SMOKED OYSTER 38
- SALMON STEAK AND CITRUS SALSA 40
- HEAVENLY SMOKED COD 43
- SWEET SMOKED SALMON 45
- OFFBEAT SCOTTISH CULLEN SKINK 47
- SALMON ON ALDER PLANK 49

CHAPTER 4: VEGETABLE RECIPES 51
Tender Soft Balsamic Cabbage 51
Divine Smoked Cauliflower 53
Lovely Paprika Corn 55
Feisty Smoked Artichokes 57
Terrific Pizza Jalapeno Poppers 59

CHAPTER 5: CHICKEN RECIPES 61
Juicy Crawfish Stuffed Chicken Breast 61
Beer Dredged Fascinating Chicken 64
Crispy Orange Chicken 66
Chicken Guacamole Pita 68
Cool Mesquite Bacon Chicken 70

CHAPTER 6: TURKEY RECIPES 72
Smoked Turkey With Onions And Apples 72
Slightly Spiced Turkey Legs 74

CHAPTER 7: GAME RECIPES 76
Fantastic Smoked Game Hens 76
Luxurious Smoked Rabbit 78
Pleasant Garlic Smoked Pheasant 80
Ultimate Smoke Quail 82

MASTERBUILT SMOKER TIPS 84
Looking at the History of Masterbuilt 84
Familiarizing Yourself With The Terms Of Smoking 85
Advantages of Using Masterbuilt Smokers 87
Why Choose Masterbuilt? 88
The Top 3 Masterbuilt Smokers To Look For 89
Buying The Right Smoker 92
Learning To Use The Masterbuilt Controls 93
Some Healthy Tips 95

SMOKE AND MEAT 96
TYPES OF SMOKERS 96
ELECTRIC SMOKERS 96
GAS SMOKERS 96
CHARCOAL SMOKERS 96
PALLET SMOKERS 96
TYPES OF SMOKER WOODS 98
THE DIFFERENT TYPES OF CHARCOAL AND THEIR BENEFITS 100
LUMP CHARCOAL: 100
CHARCOAL BRIQUETTES: 100
THE DIFFERENCE BETWEEN BARBECUING A MEAT AND SMOKING IT?
.... 101
BARBECUING MEAT: 101
SMOKING MEAT: 101
THE CORE DIFFERENCE BETWEEN COLD AND HOT SMOKING 103
THE CORE ELEMENTS OF SMOKING 104
THE BASIC PREPARATIONS FOR SMOKING MEAT 105
CHOOSING SMOKER 105
CHOOSING FUEL 105
TYPE OF SMOKING METHOD 105
SOAKING CHIPS OF WOOD 105
SET SMOKER 105
SELECTING MEAT FOR SMOKING 106
GETTING MEAT READY 106
PLACING MEAT INTO THE SMOKER 106
BASTING MEAT 107

CONCLUSION 108
GET YOUR FREE GIFT 109
OTHER BOOKS BY DANIEL MURRAY 110

AN INTRODUCTION TO SMOKED FOOD

Through history, smoking been a preferred way of preserving food, but it so much more than just a way to keep food from going bad! Smoking also introduces complex and delicious flavors into dishes that are otherwise often bland or uninteresting. In modern cooking, it's a great way to mix up staples in your home cooking, and it can be a really fantastic way to wow people at a potluck, or to host an incredible dinner party. Smoking is not only inventive and delicious, it also makes it really easy to make large quantities of food at the same time without too much fuss.

Traditionally, smoking is done by burning wood chips in a small enclosed area with the food, allowing the food to be cooked very slowly, while absorbing the rich smoky flavor.

Today, smoking is often associated with sports tailgaiting parties and small family get-togethers. This guide is designed to both embrace that culture, and also offer up some techniques and recipes that will let you take your smoking to the next level: full-blown gourmet food full of layered and nuanced deliciousness.

While Masterbuilt may not be the oldest Smoker manufacturer out there in the market, they are still around from the 1970s and knows what they are doing! Masterbuilt is a long-standing brand that has accumulated a vast reputation for being one of the top Smoker Manufacturers out there with a company that was built on faith, family and sheer hard work! This is a company that always tries to combine invention, faith and family values and tries to come up with appliances that are both robust in features and extremely easy to use for beginners. If you are reading this book, then you are probably either deciding to buy a Masterbuilt Smoker or already have purchased one and are looking for amazing recipes to explore! If you are from the latter group, you may skip the intro and jump right into the recipes! However, if you are new to Smoking, then I would highly encourage you to go through this brief yet useful introductory chapter. Throughout the following pages, I will give you an overview of Smoking and let you know how to use and adequately take care of your Masterbuilt Electric Smoker (Alongside a brief buying guide)!

Chapter 1: Beef Recipes

Mesmerizing Korean Beef Ribs

(TOTAL COOK TIME 3 HOURS)

INGREDIENTS FOR 2 SERVINGS

THE MEAT

- 1 and ½ pounds Beef short ribs

THE MARINADE

- ½ cup soy sauce
- 2 tablespoons brown sugar
- 1 tablespoon Granulated sugar

- ½ cup water
- 1-inch piece ginger, peeled and sliced
- 1 pear, ripe, peeled, cored and chopped
- 2 teaspoons sesame oil
- 1 green onion, trimmed and chopped
- 2 garlic cloves, minced
- 1 teaspoon salt

THE SMOKE

- Pre-heat your smoker to 225 degrees F
- Use Oakwoods for smoking.
- Set smoking time to 3 hours

METHOD

1. Prepare the marinade by add soy sauce, vinegar, water, granulated sugar, brown sugar, ginger, garlic, pear, green onion, salt and sesame oil in a food processor
2. Mix well until everything is combined
3. Take a re-sealable zip bag and add beef ribs
4. Add prepared marinade in the bag and toss until the rib is coated well
5. Seal plastic bag tightly and let it marinate overnight
6. Prepare your Smoker as instructed
7. Take the bag out and discard excess marinade
8. Place ribs on Smoker Tray and Smoke for 3 hours until the internal temperature reaches 165 degrees Fahrenheit
9. Serve hot with drizzle sauce
10. Enjoy

Indian Ground Beef Kebabs

(TOTAL COOK TIME 1 HOUR)

INGREDIENTS FOR 6 SERVINGS

THE MEAT

- 2 pounds Beef Sirloin, boneless

The Marinade

- 3 garlic cloves, minced
- ½ teaspoon turmeric, ground
- 2 teaspoons paprika
- 1 teaspoon kosher salt
- 1 teaspoon ground cumin
- ½ cup olive oil
- 1/3 cup red wine vinegar

The Smoke

- Pre-heat your smoker to 225 degrees F
- Use Oakwoods for smoking.
- Set smoking time to 1 hour

Method

1. Blend garlic, paprika, turmeric, cumin, pepper, red wine vinegar and salt to a food processor
2. Blend until smooth
3. Add olive oil and toss
4. Place beef cubes in a re-sealable bag and pour marinade over beef
5. Seal tightly and keep the cubes in the fridge for 2 hours, make sure to turn the bag occasionally
6. Prepare the smoker as instructed
7. Remove beef portions from the bag and discard excess marinade
8. Thread the cubes on metal/bamboo skewers
9. Smoke the Beef Kebabs until the internal temperature reaches 160 degrees F
10. Serve and enjoy!

Original Southern Barbacoa

(TOTAL COOK TIME **3** HOURS)

INGREDIENTS FOR 12 SERVINGS

The Meat

- 3 pound boneless beef chuck roast

The Rub

- 1 tablespoon dried oregano
- 1 and 1/2 teaspoons cayenne pepper
- 1 and 1/2 teaspoons chilli powder
- 1 and ½ teaspoons garlic powder
- 1 teaspoon ground cumin
- 1 teaspoon salt

The Smoke

- Pre-heat your smoker to 200 degrees F
- Use Oakwoods for smoking.
- Set smoking time to 1 and ½ hours

Method

1. Prepare the Smoker accordingly
2. Take a small bowl and add oregano, cayenne pepper, black pepper, chilli, garlic powder, cumin, salt and seasoned salt
3. Mix well and dip the chuck roast in the mixing bowl, rub the spice mix all over
4. Transfer meat to smoker and smoke for 1 and ½ hours, making sure to turn it after every 30 minutes
5. Once the edges are dark, transfer the meat to a roasting pan and seal with aluminium foil
6. Pre-heat your oven to 325 degrees F and transfer meat to the oven
7. Bake for 1 and ½ hours
8. Shred using a fork and serve!

Texas Smoked Beef Brisket

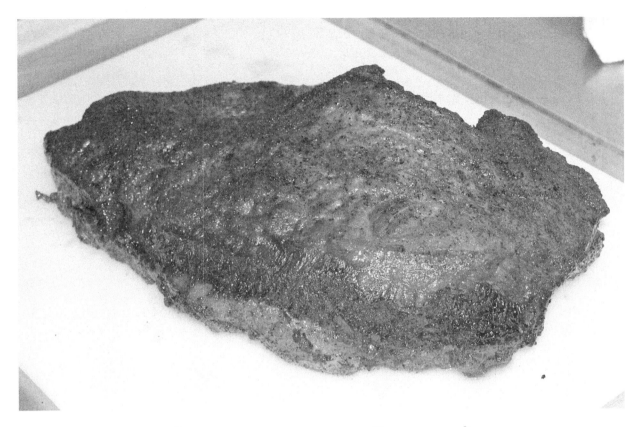

(TOTAL COOK TIME 8 HOURS)

INGREDIENTS FOR 2 SERVINGS

THE MEAT

- 14 pounds whole brisket

THE RUB

- 2 tablespoons garlic powder
- 2 tablespoons ground black pepper
- 2 tablespoons kosher salt

The Smoke

- Pre-heat your smoker to 200 degrees F
- Use Oakwoods for smoking.
- Set smoking time to 8 hours

Method

1. Remove fat/silver from the skin of brisket
2. Add garlic powder, pepper, salt to a bowl and mix
3. Season beef with a mixture
4. Prepare your smoker accordingly
5. Put beef on smoker and Smoke for 8 hours until the temperature reaches 165 degrees F
6. Remove beef from smoker and wrap in aluminium foil
7. Put beef back on Smoker and Smoke for 8 hours until the internal temperature reaches 200 degrees F
8. Remove beef from smoker and let it cool for 1 hour
9. Slice meat and serve!

BBQ Smoked Chuck

(TOTAL COOK TIME 10 HOURS)

INGREDIENTS FOR 10 SERVINGS

THE MEAT

- 5 pounds beef chuck roll

THE RUB

- 1/3 cup pepper
- ¼ cup kosher salt

The Smoke

- Pre-heat your smoker to 275 degrees F
- Use Oakwoods for smoking.
- Set smoking time to 10 hours

Method

1. Add salt and pepper to a bowl and season beef with the mix
2. Prepare your smoker accordingly
3. Place beef in your Smoker and Smoke for 4 hours until the internal temperature reaches 165 degrees F
4. Take the beef out and wrap with aluminium foil
5. Place it back to the Smoker and Smoke for 5 hours more until the temperature is 140 degrees F
6. Take it out and let it cool for 30 minutes
7. Slice and serve with onion, pickles and white bread
8. Enjoy!

Generously Smoked Beef Stew

(TOTAL COOK TIME **10** HOURS)

INGREDIENTS FOR **10** SERVINGS

THE MEAT

- 2 pounds stewing beef, cubed

THE STEW

- 5 cups beef broth
- 1 can tomatoes, diced
- 8 carrots, peeled and diced
- 8 medium potatoes, peeled and diced
- 2 onions, diced
- 2 tablespoons cornstarch
- 2 tablespoons water

THE RUB

- 1 tablespoon paprika
- 1 tablespoon sugar
- 2 teaspoon dry oregano
- 1 teaspoon garlic powder
- 1 teaspoon ground black pepper
- 1 teaspoon salt
- ½ teaspoon cayenne pepper
- ½ teaspoon thyme

THE SMOKE

- Pre-heat your smoker to 275 degrees F
- Use Oakwoods for smoking.
- Set smoking time to 10 hours

METHOD

1. Take a bowl and add the rub ingredients
2. Mix well and season the beef thoroughly
3. Prepare the Smoker accordingly
4. Put beef in Smoker and smoke for 2 hours
5. Remove beef and put in Slow Cooker
6. Add beef broth, carrots, tomatoes, potatoes and onion
7. Cook on LOW for 8 hours
8. Create a blend of cornstarch and water and add it to the Slow Cooker just 15 minutes before finishing
9. Serve with bread
10. Enjoy!

Chapter 2: Pork Recipes

The Great Andouille Sausage

(TOTAL COOK TIME 4 HOURS)

INGREDIENTS FOR 10 SERVINGS

THE MEAT

- 5 pounds pork shoulder/fresh ham

THE SEASONING

- 1 tablespoon paprika
- 1 tablespoon ground black pepper
- 1 teaspoon cayenne pepper
- 3 teaspoon salt
- 1 teaspoon cure

The Mixture

- 1 cup cold water
- 2 tablespoons garlic powder
- 2 tablespoons dried chilli flakes

The Smoke

- Pre-heat your smoker to 130 degrees F
- Use Hickory woods for smoking.
- Set smoking time to 4 hours

Method

1. Slice the pork meat and fat into 2-inch cubes
2. Grind 2/3 of the pork meat
3. Dice the remaining 1/3 pork meat into small chunks
4. Take a bowl and add the ingredients listed under seasoning
5. Add the seasoning to the meat and mix well
6. Add meat to the mixture created by mixing the ingredients listed under "mixture"
7. Stir and mix well, place it in your fridge and let it sit for 3 hours
8. Fill the sausage casings with the meat mix
9. Prepare the smoker according to the instructions above
10. Transfer sausage to your Smoker and smoke for 4 hours
11. Remove sausage from smoker and soak in hot water bath (at 165 degrees Fahrenheit) for 45 minutes
12. Remove from water bath and hang for 2 hours
13. Serve and enjoy!

Perfectly Smoke Apple BBQ Pork Belly

(TOTAL COOK TIME **8** HOURS)

INGREDIENTS FOR **8** SERVINGS

THE MEAT

- 4 pounds unseasoned pork belly, cut thick

THE GLAZE (SWEET AND SPICY RUB)

- 1 tablespoon rock sea salt
- 2 teaspoons cracked black pepper
- 2 teaspoons garlic powder
- 2 teaspoons onion powder
- 2 teaspoons smoked paprika

- 1 teaspoon ground mustard
- ½ teaspoon cayenne pepper
- ¼ cup dark brown sugar

Additional

- ½ cup BBQ sauce
- 2 cups apple juice

The Smoke

- Pre-heat your smoker to 225 degrees F
- Use Hickory woods for smoking.
- Set smoking time to 6 hours

Method

1. Prepare the smoker according to the instructions above
2. Prepare the sweet rub by mixing the ingredients listed under sweet rub, keep in a sealed container
3. Mark the top layer of your pork belly fat in 1-inch squares using a sharp knife
4. Season well with sweet rub on both sides
5. Transfer to smoker and smoke for 6 hours until the internal temperature reaches 165 degrees F, make sure to spray apple juice after every 1 hour
6. Take it out and wrap in aluminium foil with ½ cup apple juice drizzle all over
7. Seal the ends and put back in the smoker, Smoke till the internal temperature reaches 200 degrees F
8. Unwrap and discard the apple juice from the foil
9. Put the pork belly back to the smoker and glaze with BBQ sauce
10. Smoke for 10 minutes
11. Remove belly and let it cool for 15 minutes
12. Chop into cubes and serve
13. Enjoy!

Hickory Pork Loin

(TOTAL COOK TIME 3 HOURS)

INGREDIENTS FOR 4 SERVINGS

THE MEAT

- 1 whole pork loin roast

THE BRINE

- ½ quart apple juice
- ½ quart apple cider vinegar
- ½ cup sugar
- ¼ cup salt
- 2 tablespoons ground black pepper
- 2 teaspoons hickory liquid smoke

The Seasoning

- ½ cup Greek seasoning

The Smoke

- Pre-heat your smoker to 250 degrees F
- Use Hickory woods for smoking.
- Set smoking time to 3 hours

Method

1. Take a large container and prepare the brine mix by adding apple juice, vinegar, pepper, salt, sugar , liquid smoke and stir
2. Keep stirring until the liquid dissolves and add loin
3. Add more water if needed to submerge the meat
4. Cover the meat and chill overnight
5. Prepare your Smoker accordingly
6. Coat meat with Greek seasoning and transfer to Smoker
7. Smoke for 3 hours until the internal temperature reaches 160 degrees F
8. Serve and enjoy!

The Traditional "No Fuss" Pork Smoke

(TOTAL COOK TIME 8 HOURS)

INGREDIENTS FOR 8 SERVINGS

THE MEAT

- 8 pounds fresh ham

THE RUB

- ½ cup olive oil
- ¼ cup parsley, chopped
- 4 tablespoons light brown sugar
- ½ teaspoon fresh oregano
- ½ teaspoon fresh thyme
- 8 large fresh basil leaves
- 6 garlic cloves

Additional

- BBQ sauce for serving

The Smoke

- Pre-heat your smoker to 275 degrees F
- Use Hickory woods for smoking.
- Set smoking time to 6 hours

Method

1. Add the rub ingredients to a bowl (except sugar) and blend them well until thick
2. Season the ham generously with the mixture
3. Sprinkle sugar
4. Wrap in foil and place in fridge, let it sit overnight
5. Prepare the smoker accordingly and unwrap the ham
6. Transfer to your Smoker and Smoke for 6 hours until the internal temperature reaches 170 degrees F
7. Remove ham from smoker and let it cool for 20 minute
8. Serve with BBQ sauce
9. Enjoy!

All-Time Favorite Pork Jerky

(TOTAL COOK TIME 3 HOUR)

INGREDIENTS FOR 4 SERVINGS

THE MEAT

- 1 pound pork loin, centre cut

THE MARINADE

- 1 and ½ tablespoons soy sauce
- ½ teaspoon black pepper
- ½ teaspoon kosher salt
- ¼ teaspoon onion powder
- ¼ teaspoon garlic powder
- 1 pinch red pepper flakes

THE SMOKE

- Pre-heat your smoker to 225 degrees F
- Add sweet tea and water to the water tray
- Use Apple woods for smoking.
- Set smoking time to 3 hours

METHOD

1. Trim excess fat off from the pork loin and slice it in your desired size
2. Add slices to a re-sealable zip bag
3. Take a large bowl and add spices and herbs to prepare the marinade
4. Pour the marinade into the zip bag and toss to coat the pork slices, seal tightly
5. Refrigerate overnight
6. Take the bag out and let it reach room temperature
7. Prepare the Smoker accordingly
8. Remove pork pieces from plastic bag and add pieces over Smoker racks
9. Smoke for 3 hours
10. Add more chips and sweet water if needed after 1 and ½ hours
11. Once the pork is moist and not completely dry, remove and let it reach room temperature
12. Drizzle more sauce and enjoy!

Super Spicy Pork Loin With Apple Cabbage Slaw

(TOTAL COOK TIME 4 HOURS)

INGREDIENTS FOR 10 SERVINGS

THE MEAT

- 4-5 pounds pork loin, boneless

THE MARINADE

- 3 teaspoons sea salt
- 1 tablespoon Chinese five spice powder
- ½ teaspoon Garlic powder
- 1 teaspoon Black pepper
- 2 tablespoons Grapeseed
- ¼ teaspoon nutmeg

The Slaw

- ½ of a medium Green Cabbage
- ½ a medium purple cabbage
- 2 tablespoon apple cider vinegar
- 2 large Fuji apples
- 1 teaspoon sea salt
- 1 teaspoon Maple syrup
- 1 teaspoon Black pepper
- ½ cup hazelnuts, toasted, roughly chopped

The Smoke

- Pre-heat your smoker to 225 degrees F, prepare water tray by mixing apple juice and water
- Use Apple woods for smoking.
- Set smoking time to 3 hours

Method

1. Rinse pork In cold water and use kitchen towels to drain them
2. Trim excess fat and slice into pieces of ¼ inch
3. Place pork loin in lined pan
4. Take a bowl and add herbs and spices alongside oil
5. Use the mix to rub over pork and let it sit for 60 minutes
6. Prepare the smoker as instructed
7. Wash the cabbages and shred them in a big bowl
8. Slice apples and add to the bowl
9. Add maple syrup, apple cider, pepper, vinegar and salt
10. Toss well and place the bowl of slaw in fridge
11. Place marinated pork in middle rack and Smoke for 3 hours until the internal temperature reaches 155 degrees Fahrenheit
12. Make sure to keep checking the pork after every 30 minutes to add more woods, juice or water
13. Take the pork out and wrap in aluminium foil, let it rest for 20 minutes
14. Take a pan over medium heat and toast hazelnuts, roughly chop them
15. Slice pork for sandwiches and topple with apple cabbage slaw and toasted hazelnuts
16. Enjoy!

Chapter 3: Fish and Seafood Recipes

Salmon And Vodka Delight

(Total cook time 4 hours)

Ingredients for 4 servings

The Meat

- 1 pound Salmon fillet, bones and skins removed

The Rub

- ¼ cup kosher salt
- ¼ cup brown Turbinado sugar
- 2 tablespoons black pepper
- 1 bunch fresh dill, chopped
- ½ thinly sliced lemon

The Soak

- 1 shot vodka, unflavored

The Smoke

- Use Alder woods for smoking.
- Set smoking time to 4 hours

Method

1. Prepare your fish by cutting it in half and stacking them on top of each other
2. Take a glass tray and fill with vodka
3. Add salmon fillets to the vodka and rub the surface with salt, pepper and sugar
4. Gently press down dill on surface salmon and wrap with plastic
5. Wrap them with one more layer and leave in the fridge for 12 hours
6. After 12 hours, remove the fish tray from the fridge and discard the liquid
7. Clean fillet using cold water and remove rubbed seasoning
8. Clean the fillets using a kitchen towel and keep them on the side for 2 hours
9. Prepare your smoker as instructed above
10. Rub olive oil on the smoker grate and place fillets on the smoker
11. Smoke for 4 hours, making sure to keep adding wood chips after every 45 minutes
12. Make sure to check the doneness after 2 and ½ hours as fish tend to get cooked soon. The internal temperature should be 135 degrees F once done
13. Take it out from the smoker and let it sit for 15 minutes
14. Serve and enjoy!

Lovely Smoked Shrimp

(TOTAL COOK TIME 1 HOUR)

INGREDIENTS FOR 25 SERVINGS

THE MEAT

- 4 pounds shrimps, headless – shell on

THE DRY RUB

- 1/8 cup black pepper
- 1 tablespoon sweet basil
- 1 tablespoon oregano
- 1 teaspoon cumin
- 1 teaspoon paprika
- 1 teaspoon nutmeg

THE SOAK

- 1 and ½ sticks butter
- 1/3 cup Worcestershire sauce
- ¼ cup hot sauce
- 1 teaspoon liquid crab boil

THE SMOKE

- Pre-heat your smoker to 230 degrees F
- Use the Pecan/Apple woods for smoking.
- Set smoking time to 60 minutes

METHOD

1. Melt butter in Smoker Safe pan in your microwave
2. Remove pan from smoker and pour Worcestershire sauce, crab oil and hot sauce
3. Add 25 shrimps to the pan and coat it thoroughly
4. Take the dry ingredients in another bowl and mix, sprinkle over shrimp
5. Use your hand to mix the shrimps well
6. Prepare your Smoker as instructed above
7. Place shrimp in your Smoker and smoke until they are opaque and curled up, should take about 60 minutes
8. Turn the shrimp from time to time during cooking
9. After 60 minutes, spoon out the shrimp from pan and transfer to a platter
10. Pour extra sauce and serve
11. Enjoy!

Gentle Smoked Trout

(TOTAL COOK TIME **1-2** HOURS)

INGREDIENTS FOR **6** SERVINGS

THE MEAT

- 10-12 trout fillets

THE MARINADE

- ½ cup soy sauce
- 2 teaspoons salt
- Garlic salt as needed
- 1 teaspoon dill seeds
- 4 cups water
- ½ cup teriyaki sauce
- 2 teaspoons lemon pepper

THE SMOKE

- Pre-heat your Smoker to 225 degrees F
- Use Alder woods for smoking.
- Set smoking time to 2 hours

METHOD

1. Take a bowl and add all of the listed ingredients
2. Mix well and add the trout fillets
3. Let them refrigerate overnight
4. Remove fillets from the fridge just 1 hour before smoking
5. Prepare your Smoker accordingly
6. Place fillets in middle rack and Smoke for 1-2 hours until the internal temperature of the fillets reaches 145 degrees F
7. Serve and enjoy!

Pacific Smoked Oyster

(TOTAL COOK TIME 2 HOURS)

INGREDIENTS FOR 8 SERVINGS

THE MEAT

- 40-50 Oysters, in shells

THE STEAM SOLUTION

- 1 cup white wine
- 1 cup water

THE DRIZZLE

- ¼ cup extra virgin olive oil

THE SMOKE

- Pre-heat your Smoker to 145 degrees F
- Use Cherry woods for smoking.
- Set smoking time to 2 hours

METHOD

1. Wash oysters under cold water
2. Take a bowl and add white wine, water and bring the mix to a boil
3. Add oysters in a single layer and steam for 3 minutes until they are open
4. Transfer opened oysters to a bowl and add more to the steaming pot, keep repeating until all the oysters are used
5. Strain the cooking liquid through a paper towel into a bowl and keep it on the side
6. Take a small bowl and use a sharp knife to remove the oysters from shells, transfer oysters to the bowl
7. Dip remove oysters in the strained cooking liquid for 20 minutes
8. Prepare the Smoker accordingly
9. Transfer oyster to middle rack and Smoke for 1 and ½ to 2 hours
10. Drizzle olive oil over oysters and serve
11. Enjoy!

Salmon Steak And Citrus Salsa

(TOTAL COOK TIME **1** HOUR)

INGREDIENTS FOR **4** SERVINGS

THE MEAT

- 4 salmon steaks, boneless

THE RUB

- 1 teaspoon black pepper
- ½ teaspoon sea salt
- 2 limes, juiced
- ½ lemon, juiced
- 1 tablespoon brown sugar
- 1 tablespoon basil, chopped

THE SALSA

- 3 cups papaya, peeled and diced
- 2 cups pineapple, diced
- 1 cup mango, chopped
- 2 tablespoons cilantro, chopped
- ½ cup green onion, chopped
- ½ teaspoon salt
- 2 tablespoons lime juice
- 1 tablespoon sugar

THE SMOKE

- Pre-heat your smoker to 230 degrees F
- Use the Pecan/Apple woods for smoking.
- Set smoking time to 1 hour

Method

1. Take a bowl and add pepper, salt, lemon juice, basil and brown sugar
2. Reserve half of this marinade for later use
3. Place salmon in a dish and cover with the marinade
4. Refrigerate for 30-45 minutes
5. Prepare the Smoker as instructed above and place the marinated salmon in the middle rack of the Smoker
6. Smoke for 45-60 minutes, making sure to keep brushing it with the marinade
7. Add more chips if needed
8. Take a medium sized bowl and add pineapple, mango, papaya, green onion, lime juice, sugar and salt
9. Mix well
10. Take the Salmon out and keep it on the side, let it rest until it reaches room temperature
11. Serve the Salmon topped with citrus salsa
12. Enjoy!

Heavenly Smoked Cod

(TOTAL COOK TIME **1** HOUR)

INGREDIENTS FOR **4** SERVINGS

THE MEAT

- 10-12 cod fillets

THE MARINADE

- ½ cup soy sauce
- 2 teaspoons salt
- Garlic salt as needed
- 1 teaspoon dill seeds
- 4 cups water
- ½ cup teriyaki sauce
- 2 teaspoons lemon pepper

The Smoke

- Pre-heat your smoker to 225 degrees F
- Use the Pecan/Apple woods for smoking.
- Set smoking time to 1 hour

Method

1. Take a bowl and add all the listed ingredients
2. Toss it well to coat the fish
3. Let it refrigerate overnight
4. Prepare the smoker according to the instructions above
5. Place fillets in the middle rack of your Smoker and Smoke until the internal temperature reaches 145 degrees F
6. Serve and enjoy!

Sweet Smoked Salmon

(TOTAL COOK TIME **1-2** HOURS)

INGREDIENTS FOR **6** SERVINGS

THE MEAT

- 5 pounds salmon fillets, cut into 6-ounce chunks

THE MARINADE

- 1 heaping cup brown sugar
- 2 cups kosher salt
- 5-6 cups soy sauce
- 1 tablespoon pepper powder
- ½ cup honey

THE SMOKE

- Pre-heat your Smoker to 160 degrees F
- Use Alder woods for smoking.
- Set smoking time to 2 hours

METHOD

1. Place Salmon in a dish and sprinkle salt over it, toss well
2. Cover and refrigerate in your fridge for 14 hours
3. Remove dish from fridge and shake off salt mix from the strips, wipe them clean
4. Take a bowl and add remaining ingredients and pour the mixture over Salmon
5. Cover and let it marinate for 1 day
6. Prepare your Smoker accordingly
7. Grease the racks with little oil and place Salmon on the middle rack
8. Smoke for 1-2 hours until flaky
9. Serve and enjoy!

Offbeat Scottish Cullen Skink

(TOTAL COOK TIME 1 HOUR)

INGREDIENTS FOR 6 SERVINGS

THE MEAT

- 2 pounds smoked fish fillets (use any smoked fish recipe from this book)

THE SOUP

- 2 bay leaves
- 4 ounces butter
- 16 ounces mashed potatoes
- ½ cup flat leaf parsley, separate leaves and finely chopped
- 2 medium onions, finely chopped
- Salt as needed
- Pepper as needed

Method

1. Take a large saucepan and place it over medium heat
2. Add milk and add stalk parsley, bay leaf and smoked fish
3. Bring it to a boil for a couple minutes and remove heat
4. Let it sit for 10 minutes
5. Remove fish with a slotted spoon and keep it on the side
6. Strain milk by passing through a wire mesh strainer, keep it on the side
7. Place a large saucepan over medium heat and add butter, let the butter melt
8. Add onions and Saute until translucent
9. Add strained milk into the pan
10. Add mashed potatoes and mix
11. Discard bones of fish and flake the fish
12. Add into the saucepan
13. Add parsley leaves and simmer for 5-10 minutes
14. Season with salt and pepper and let it simmer for a few minutes more
15. Ladle into soup bowls and serve
16. Enjoy!

Salmon on Alder Plank

(TOTAL COOK TIME 2 HOURS)

INGREDIENTS FOR 10 SERVINGS

THE MEAT

- 3 pounds salmon fillets

THE SEASONING

- Fresh ground black pepper
- 1/8 cup brown sugar
- ½ teaspoon salt
- 1 tablespoon water

The Brine

- 1-gallon water
- 4 cups salt

Smoke

- Pre-heat your Smoker to 160 degrees F
- Use Alder woods for smoking.
- Set smoking time to 2 hours

Method

1. Soak the fillets in a brine water for 4 hours
2. Take another bucket of water and submerge alder wood plank
3. Prepare your Smoker accordingly
4. Take salmon out from brine solution and rinse well
5. Pat dry with kitchen towels
6. Take out the wood planks and lay Salmon on top
7. Season with salt and pepper
8. Place in the middle rack of your Smoker and Smoke for 2 hours until flaky
9. Take a bowl and mix water and brown sugar and baste the salmon during the final 30 minutes of cooking
10. Serve and enjoy!

Chapter 4: Vegetable Recipes

Tender Soft Balsamic Cabbage

(TOTAL COOK TIME 2 HOURS)

INGREDIENTS FOR 4 SERVINGS

THE VEGETABLE

- 1 small head green cabbage

THE SEASONING

- ½ teaspoon salt
- ½ teaspoon black pepper
- 2 tablespoon butter
- Extra virgin olive oil
- 1 tablespoon sugar

The Smoke

- Pre-heat your smoker to 225 degrees F
- Use Mesquite woods for smoking.
- Set smoking time to 2 hours

Method

1. Prepare the Smoker as instructed above
2. Remove outer leaves of the cabbage and wash it well
3. Take a sharp knife and remove the core
4. Take a small bowl and add vinegar, salt, pepper and butter
5. Stir well and pour the mixture into the hole in the cabbage (created by removing the core)
6. Drizzle olive oil and add seasoning
7. Place onto a baking pan (cut side facing up)
8. Place baking pan into your Smoker and Smoke for 1-2 hours
9. Add more chips if needed
10. Remove cabbage and cover with foil, return back to smoker and smoke for 30 minutes more
11. Serve and enjoy!

Divine Smoked Cauliflower

(TOTAL COOK TIME 2 HOURS)

INGREDIENTS FOR 4 SERVINGS

THE VEGETABLE

- 1 head cauliflower

THE SEASONING

- Olive oil
- Salt as needed
- Pepper as needed
- 2 teaspoon dried oregano
- 2 teaspoon dried basil

THE SMOKE

- Pre-heat your smoker to 200 degrees F
- Use Mesquite woods for smoking.
- Set smoking time to 2 hours

METHOD

1. Prepare the Smoker as instructed above
2. Take the cauliflower to a chopping board and cut into medium-sized pieces
3. Remove the core and place the cauliflowers onto a sheet pan
4. Drizzle olive oil
5. Sprinkle seasoning and herbs all over
6. Place them in your Smoker and Smoke for 2 hours, making sure to turn them often
7. Serve and enjoy!

Lovely Paprika Corn

(TOTAL COOK TIME 2 HOURS)

INGREDIENTS FOR 26 SERVINGS

THE VEGETABLE

- As many Corn on Cob as you want (Depending on your preference)

THE SEASONING

- Olive oil
- Paprika, according to your taste
- Salt as needed
- Pepper as needed

The Smoke

- Pre-heat your smoker to 200 degrees F
- Use Mesquite woods for smoking.
- Set smoking time to 1 hour 30 minutes

Method

1. Prepare the Smoker as instructed above
2. Peel the outer leaves from your corn and remove any stringy bits
3. Keep them on the side
4. Take a small bowl and add olive oil, a pinch of paprika, pepper and salt
5. Brush the mix generously over corn
6. Transfer the corn inside your Smoker and Smoke for 90 minutes, making sure to open after every 30 minutes to turn the cobs and brush them with more paprika oil
7. Serve and enjoy once ready

Feisty Smoked Artichokes

(TOTAL COOK TIME **1** HOUR)

INGREDIENTS FOR **4** SERVINGS

THE VEGETABLE

- Steamed Artichokes, 4 medium globes, halved

The Seasoning

- ½ cup extra virgin olive oil
- 1 lemon, juice
- 4 garlic cloves, minced
- Salt and pepper as needed

The Smoke

- Pre-heat your smoker to 200 degrees F
- Use Mesquite woods for smoking.
- Set smoking time to 1 hour

Method

1. Prepare the Smoker as instructed above
2. Add garlic, lemon juice, olive oil to a small bowls
3. Season to taste
4. Stir well and use the mixture to glaze the Steamed artichoke halves
5. Transfer them to the Smoker bottom rack
6. Smoke for 1 hour
7. Serve and enjoy!

Terrific Pizza Jalapeno Poppers

(TOTAL COOK TIME 1 HOUR)

INGREDIENTS FOR 6 SERVINGS

THE VEGETABLE

- 12 large Jalapeno peppers

THE SEASONING

- 8-ounce cream cheese
- 4-ounce cheddar cheese, shredded
- 4-ounce mozzarella cheese, shredded
- Bred heel, 2 slices
- 12 bacon slices

THE SMOKE

- Pre-heat your smoker to 200 degrees F
- Use Mesquite woods for smoking.
- Set smoking time to 1 hour

METHOD

1. Prepare the Smoker as instructed above
2. Add the cheeses to a food processor and blend until smooth
3. Cut stems off the peppers and scoop out seeds
4. Fill the inside with cheese mix
5. Tear a small piece of bread from crusts and add them to the cut end of the pepper to avoid cheese oozing out
6. Wrap bacon around the peppers and secure them using a toothpick
7. Place directly in your smoker and smoke for 30-60 minutes
8. Make sure to check after 30 minutes for doneness
9. Serve and enjoy!

Chapter 5: Chicken Recipes

Juicy Crawfish Stuffed Chicken Breast

(Total cook time 2 hours)

Ingredients for 4 servings

The Meat

- 4 chicken breast, boneless
- 1 cup crawfish, pre-cooked, chopped

The Stuffing

- 1/3 cup bell red bell pepper, chopped
- ¼ cup green onion, chopped
- 1/3 cup parsley, chopped
- 1 cup cheese blend, shredded
- ½ cup mayonnaise
- ½ teaspoons Cajun hot sauce
- ½ cup Moppin' Sauce

The Rub

- 1-2 teaspoons Cajun seasoning

The Smoke

- Preheat a smoker to 275 degrees F prior to smoking.
- Use Sassafras woods for smoking.
- Set smoking time to 2 hours

Method

1. Take a large pot and add ½ gallon water, kosher salt, brown sugar. Add the chicken breast and leave it in your fridge for the whole night
2. Take the breasts out and dry them using a paper towel
3. Leave the chicken on the side
4. Prepare to stuff by taking a large bowl and add crawfish, red pepper, green onion, cheese, parsley, hot sauce and mayonnaise
5. Mix well
6. Wrap the breast using plastic film and beat using a mallet to soften it
7. Remove the film and sprinkle Cajun seasoning, rub it nicely
8. Take the stuffing and place it on top of the breast
9. Roll the breast and seal it nicely
10. Prepare the smoker as directed above and insert the rolled Cajun-seasoned chicken breast
11. Smoke until the internal temperature reaches 160 degrees F
12. Cook for 30 minutes more until the temperature reaches 165 degrees F
13. After 30 minutes, remove the breast and keep it on the side for 10-15 minutes
14. Serve and enjoy!

Beer Dredged Fascinating Chicken

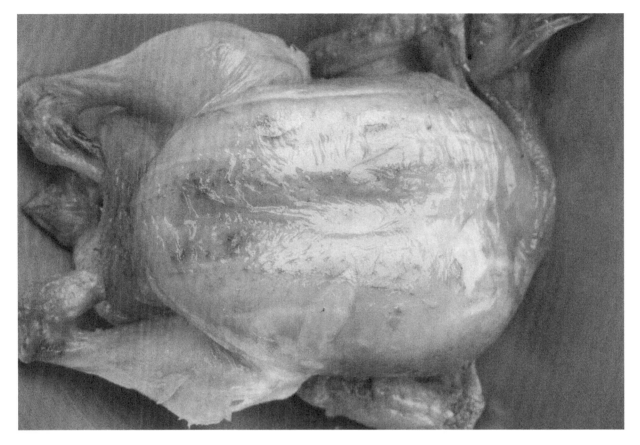

(TOTAL COOK TIME 2 HOURS)

INGREDIENTS FOR 6 SERVINGS

THE MEAT

- 1 whole chicken (3 pounds)

The Marinade

- ½ cup Rice Vinegar
- ½ cup apple juice concentrate
- 3 tablespoon natural ketchup
- 1 piece (2 inches) ginger, grated
- 2 tablespoons Dijon mustard
- 2 tablespoons olive oil
- ¼ teaspoon black pepper, ground
- 1 lemon, zest and juice
- 1 beer can

The Smoke

- Preheat a smoker to 250 degrees F prior to smoking and set the mode to Direct.
- Use Apple woods for smoking.
- Set smoking time to 2 hours

Method

1. Take a mixing bowl and add the listed ingredients under marinade
2. Take the chicken and carefully empty the cavity
3. Rinse it with cold water and dry it well
4. Use the marinade to cover the chicken and place it in your fridge for 2 hours (for more flavour, keep it for 24 hours)
5. Take the chicken out and remove from marinade, keep the remaining marinade for later use
6. Prepare the smoker as instructed above
7. Place chicken on the rack and use a drip pan filled up with beer and water
8. Smoke the chicken for doneness until the temperature reaches 185 degrees F
9. Serve and enjoy!

Crispy Orange Chicken

(TOTAL COOK TIME 1 AND 1/2 - 2 HOURS)

INGREDIENTS FOR 4 SERVINGS

THE MEAT

- 4 quarter chicken

THE SPICE RUB

- 4 teaspoons paprika
- 1 tablespoon chilli powder
- 2 teaspoons ground cumin
- 2 teaspoons dried thyme
- 2 teaspoons salt
- 2 teaspoons garlic powder
- 1 teaspoon fresh ground black pepper

THE MARINADE

- 2 cups frozen orange juice concentrate
- ½ cup soy sauce
- 1 tablespoon garlic powder

THE SMOKE

- Pre-heat your smoker to 275 degrees F
- Use Apple woods for smoking.
- Set smoking time to 2 hours

METHOD

1. Take a small bowl and add the seasoning ingredients, mix well
2. Transfer chicken quarters to a large dish
3. Take a medium bowl and whisk in the marinade ingredients and half of the spice mix
4. Pour marinade over chicken and cover, refrigerate for 8 hours
5. Prepare your Smoker accordingly
6. Discard marinade and rub the chicken surface with remaining spice rub
7. Transfer chicken to smoker and smoke for 1 and ½ to 2 hours until the internal temperature reaches 160 degrees F
8. Let it rest for 10 minutes
9. Serve and enjoy!

Chicken Guacamole Pita

(TOTAL COOK TIME 1 HOUR)

INGREDIENTS FOR 5-6 SERVINGS

THE MEAT

- 2 pieces chicken breast

THE RUB

- Salt as needed
- Pepper as needed
- Cajun seasoning according to taste

THE GUACAMOLE

- 2 avocados, ripe
- 1 small onion, diced
- 1 small tomato, diced
- 1 lime

THE SMOKE

- Preheat your Smoker to 225 degrees Fahrenheit
- Use Pecan woods for smoking.
- Set smoking time to 1 hour

METHOD

1. Prepare your Smoker as instructed above
2. Take your desired amount of Cajun seasoning and rub it over chicken breast pieces and season them carefully
3. Place meat in a lined pan and transfer to your Smoker
4. Smoke for 1 hour until the internal temperature reaches 165 degrees F
5. While the chicken is smoking, prepare the guacamole
6. Take a chopping board and cut the avocado in half lengthwise
7. Remove seed. Use a spoon to scoop out the flesh and add to a bowl
8. Cut a lime in half and squeeze over the avocado
9. Mix well
10. Slice tomato lengthwise and remove seed, dice the tomato
11. Chop onion similarly
12. Add chopped onions and tomatoes to your avocado mix and stir
13. Stir the other half of the lemon and mix
14. Take the smoker chicken out and slice it
15. Place the slices in pita bread and serve with guacamole
16. Enjoy!

Cool Mesquite Bacon Chicken

(TOTAL COOK TIME 2 HOURS)

INGREDIENTS FOR 7 SERVINGS

THE MEAT

- 4 chicken breast, skinless and boneless
- 12 slices uncooked bacon

The Seasoning

- Salt as needed
- Fresh ground black pepper

The Rub

- 1-2 teaspoons Cajun seasoning

The Butter Mix

- 1 cup maple syrup
- ½ cup melted butter
- 1 teaspoon liquid smoke

The Smoke

- Preheat a smoker to 250 degrees F prior to smoking.
- Use Mesquite woods for smoking.
- Set smoking time to 2 hours

Method

1. Prepare your smoker accordingly
2. Season chicken with salt and pepper
3. Wrap breast with 3 bacon slices, and cover the entire surface
4. Secure bacon with toothpick
5. Take a medium bowl and add maple syrup, butter, liquid smoke and mix
6. Reserve 1/3 of the mix for later use
7. Submerge prepare breast in the marinade and coat
8. Place a pan in your Smoker and transfer chicken
9. Smoke for 1 to 1 -2 hours
10. Brush chicken with reserved butter mix during the final 30 minutes of smoking until the internal temperature reaches 165 degrees F

CHAPTER 6: TURKEY RECIPES

Smoked Turkey With Onions And Apples

(TOTAL COOK TIME **11** HOURS)

INGREDIENTS FOR **4** SERVINGS

THE MEAT

- 10 pounds whole turkey, cleaned

The Marinade

- 4 garlic cloves, crushed
- 1 tablespoon garlic powder
- 2 tablespoons seasoned salt
- 1 apple, quartered
- 1 onion, quartered
- 2 x 12-ounce cans of cola
- 1 tablespoon alt
- ½ cup butter
- 1 tablespoon ground black pepper

The Smoke

- Pre-heat your smoker to 250 degrees F
- Use Maple woods for smoking.
- Set smoking time to 11 hours

Method

1. Prepare the Smoker accordingly
2. Clean the turkey and dry it
3. Rub garlic over outside and sprinkle salt
4. Transfer turkey to roasting pan
5. Take a medium bowl and add garlic, onion, apple, butter and cola, season it with salt and stir
6. Pour butter mixture into turkey and cover with foil
7. Smoke for 10 hours, making sure to check often and baste it with the juices from the pan
8. The final internal temperature of Turkey should be 180 degrees F
9. Take it out and let it sit for 30 minutes

Slightly Spiced Turkey Legs

(TOTAL COOK TIME 7 HOURS)

INGREDIENTS FOR 4 SERVINGS

THE MEAT

- 8 turkey legs

THE RUB

- ¼ cup chipotle seasoning
- 1-2 tablespoon mild dried ground red chilli
- 1 tablespoon brown sugar

The Brine

- 1-gallon water
- ½ cup sugar
- 1 cup salt

The Smoke

- Pre-heat your smoker to 250 degrees F
- Use Maple woods for smoking.
- Set smoking time to 6 hours

Method

1. Take a bowl and prepare the brine mix by adding salt, sugar and water
2. Stir well to dissolve
3. Add turkey into liquid and place it in your fridge overnight
4. Prepare the Smoker accordingly
5. Remove turkey legs from bringing mix and pat them dry
6. Rub spice mix all over turkey legs and coat them well
7. Transfer to your Smoker and smoke for 4-6 hours until crispy brown
8. Once the internal temperature reaches 180 degrees F, take them out and cover with silver foil
9. Let them rest for 15 minutes
10. Serve and enjoy!

Chapter 7: Game Recipes

Fantastic Smoked Game Hens

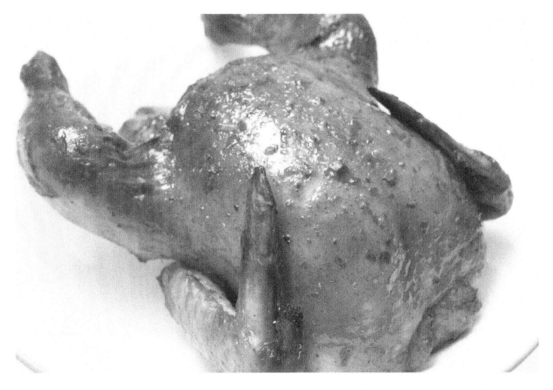

(Total cook time 2 hours 50 minutes)

Ingredients for 8 servings

The Meat

- 1 Whole Hen, halved

The Seasoning

- 1//4 cup extra virgin olive oil
- 3 quarters oranges
- 4 teaspoon salt
- 2 teaspoon cracked black pepper
- 2 teaspoon dried thyme

THE SMOKE

- Preheat a smoker to 250 degrees F prior to smoking and set the mode to Direct.
- Use Fruitwood woods for smoking.
- Set smoking time to 3 hours

METHOD

1. Clean the hens and rinse them with water
2. Dry with paper towel
3. Allow the hens to stay at room temperature for 30 minutes
4. Prepare to season by mixing the ingredients under seasoning
5. Prepare the smoker as instructed above
6. Combine the seasoning with olive oil and rub it in the cavity of each hen
7. Stuff the hen with 3 oranges quarters and tie legs with twine
8. Place hens on your Smoker rack and tuck their wings under the trunk
9. Smoke for 2 hours 30 minutes until the internal temperature reaches 165 degrees F
10. Make sure to keep adding woodchips after every 30 minutes
11. Remove hen and let them rest for 20 minutes
12. Discard organs and cut the hen in half
13. Serve and enjoy!

Luxurious Smoked Rabbit

(TOTAL COOK TIME 2 HOURS)

INGREDIENTS FOR 5 SERVINGS

THE MEAT

- 1 cottontail, skinned and gutted

THE RUB

- 1 tablespoon garlic powder
- 1 tablespoon cayenne pepper
- 1 tablespoon salt
- 1 Bottle BBQ sauce

The Brine

- ½ cup white vinegar
- 2 tablespoon kosher salt
- Water as needed

Smoke

- Pre-heat your Smoker to 200 degrees F
- Use Apple woods for smoking.
- Set smoking time to 2 hours

Method

1. Take a bowl and add salt and white vinegar to make a brine solution
2. Transfer bring to a shallow dish and add the rabbit with enough water to cover the whole rabbit
3. Let it sit for 1 hour
4. Prepare the Smoker accordingly
5. Take a bowl and whisk garlic powder, pepper, salt, cayenne pepper and rub the rabbi with the mixture generously
6. Transfer rabbit to your Smoker and smoke for 2 hours
7. Remove rabbit and serve hot
8. Enjoy!

Pleasant Garlic Smoked Pheasant

(TOTAL COOK TIME 3-4 HOURS)

INGREDIENTS FOR 8 SERVINGS

THE MEAT

- 2 whole pheasants

THE RUB

- 2 tablespoon cayenne pepper
- 4 tablespoons olive oil
- 2 tablespoons black pepper
- 2 tablespoons onion powder
- 2 teaspoons paprika
- 2 garlic clove, crushed

THE BRINE

- 1-gallon water
- 1 cup sugar
- ¾ cup salt

THE SMOKE

- Pre-heat your smoker to 250 degrees F
- Use Maple woods for smoking.
- Set smoking time to 4 hours

METHOD

1. Take a large bowl and add salt, sugar and water, stir until dissolved
2. Place pheasant into the liquid and let it stay in the fridge overnight
3. Remove the pheasant from brine mix and let it dry
4. Prepare the Smoker accordingly
5. Take a bowl and add the spice and mix, spread over the pheasants both inside and out
6. Place pheasant in your smoker and smoke for 3-3 and ½ hours until the internal temperature reaches 180 degrees F
7. Remove from smoker and let it rest for 20-30 minutes
8. Serve and enjoy!

Ultimate Smoke Quail

(TOTAL COOK TIME **1** HOUR)

INGREDIENTS FOR **8** SERVINGS

THE MEAT

- 4-6 quails

THE RUB

- 2 tablespoons olive oil
- Salt and black pepper as needed
- 1 pack Hidden valley ranch dressing
- ½ cup melted butter

THE SMOKE

- Pre-heat your smoker to 225 degrees F
- Use Maple woods for smoking.
- Set smoking time to 1 hour

METHOD

1. Prepare the Smoker accordingly
2. Brush quail with olive oil and season with salt and pepper
3. Place in your smoker and smoke for 1 hour
4. Brush the quail with ranch mix after the 30 minutes mark and baste again at the end of the cook time
5. Once the internal temperature of quail reaches 145 degrees F
6. Serve and enjoy!

MASTERBUILT SMOKER TIPS

Looking at the History of Masterbuilt

The history behind the core concept of Masterbuilt Smokers came when an individual named Dawson McLemore took a leap of Faith and decided to pursue his passion fully!

He took his time to eventually turn his sheer desire of welding into a full-fledged family business that he ran from the backyard of his building.

He eventually caught the eye of Goodyear Tire And Rubber Company who turned him into a paid employee and provided him with a steady source of income. This source of stability gave him the foundation and courage he needed to explore his passion further and seek out new opportunities to help him and his family.

One crucial fact that makes Dawson so unique from the other contemporaries is the fact that he was a very religious man, a man of faith if you will. He operated his whole life depends on the control of the Holy One.

And according to him, the name "Masterbuilt Electric Smoker" came to him during one of his praying sessions where he was asking for guidance over his business endeavours.

Therefore, it's safe to say that the name "Masterbuilt" actually holds a very significant religious and sentimental value to Dawson! It implies that his company was not built through the inspiration of man, but built through the divine guidance of God Himself.

At the heart of all the operations that take place under the Masterbuilt roof, is family values. And all employees work upholding this tradition while trying to make their devices as accessible and family-friendly as possible.

Familiarizing Yourself With The Terms Of Smoking

Just like any hobby or "Craft" out there, the technique of smoking also comes with its fair share of unique words and vocabulary that may seem slightly confusing to an untrained ear.
So, let me educate you a little bit on this topic so that things don't seem that confusing moving forward!
I will try to explain the various terms as quickly and just as possible. Let's cover the basics first.

Barbecuing: BBQ-ing is usually done on a grill! But rather than going for extreme temperatures, Barbecuing is done at a low temperature of about 300-500 degree F as opposed to grilling.

Grilling: Grilling, on the other hand, requires a high temperature that generally falls North of 500 degrees. This is rather quick cooking meat that sears the outside of the meat and seals the juice inside giving a dark, succulent finish.

Smoking: Smoking is usually done are even lower heating conditions, around 140 degrees F in some cases and is done by exposing the ingredients to smoke over a prolonged period. However, you should know that there are two types of Smoking and there is a slight difference between them.

In Hot Smoking, the Smoker simultaneously roasts and smokes the meat at temperatures above 140 degrees F, in this case, the foods are thoroughly cooked.
In Cold Smoking, however, sublet ingredients such as cheese fish prepared at shallow temperatures that fall around 69-90 degree F.
Now asides from the basics terminologies mentioned above, there are a few more that might pop up now and then. So, it's better to have a look at them as well.

AMNPS: This is a patented shorthand that stands for Amaze-N-Pellet Smoker, which is a portable smoke generator that burns either pellets or sawdust and is usable for both cold and hot smoking.

Bark: This is the name given to the crunchy fatty crust that develops outside meat after its heated past 300 degrees F, setting off a Maillard Reaction (more on this later).

Brine: This is the salting process of meat. You can either go for "wet brine," which is salt mixed with water and spices or "Dry Brine" which is merely rubbing the salt directly into the food. Brining meat helps to keep the meat moist during the smoking process.

Chimney: This is a cylindrical device that helps to ignite charcoal without lighter fluid.

COS: This stands for CHEAPO OFFSET SMOKER

Dalmatian Rub: A simple rub made of salt and pepper

EOS: This stands for EXPENSIVE OFFSET SMOKER

Gasser: A derogatory term used for propane-fueled smokers that are usually applied by those individuals who think that electric and gas-fueled smokers are "Inferior."

I.P: Liquid propane gas used to fuel smokers and grills. These are usually available in bottles of 20 pounds.

Maillard Reaction: This is a chemical process that occurs between 285-330 degree F and is responsible for providing foods with a crunchy layer of fat known as "Bark."

Montreal-Style Smoked Meat: This kind of meat is usually made by salting beef brisket and curing it with salt and spices, followed by a session of hot smoke and steam.

Reverse Sear: in this scenario, indirect heat is used to raise the temperature in the centre of the meat.

Smoke Point: This is the point at which "Fat" begins to smoke and will vary from one ingredient to the next. For example, butter has a low Smoke Point (325 degrees F) while ghee has a higher smoke point of 485 degrees F.

Stick Burner: This is a smoker that is designed to used burning logs as fuel.

Advantages of Using Masterbuilt Smokers

Masterbuilt Smokers, or any Electric Smokers for that matter, are well known for their versatility and ease of use.

As such, they pack a good number of advantages as opposed to other regular Smokers that you should be aware of.

Cleaner Energy: When using charcoal or gas as the primary source of heat, the smokers tend to generate a significant amount of dirty that negatively impact the climate and contribute to global warming. This is also the reason why many townhouses and apartments often restrict individuals from using charcoal or gas smokers. Electric Smokers, on the other hand, are very friendly in this term as they use electricity to generate the heat, release fewer toxins in the air.

Gives you time to relax: Traditional Smokers often require you to manually regulate the temperature over the Smoking session by continually feeding it fuel. Electric Smokers such as Masterbuilt saves you from this trouble as their temperature always remains consistent throughout the cooking session. You can only set it and forget it! This frees up a lot of time and allows you to spend more time doing the other things that you love.

Helps conserve energy: As hard it is to believe, Electric Smokers don't use too much electricity. An approximate count would be 800 Watts per hour. Very little heat is lost during the cooking process as the enclosure is usually built with thick steel, especially in Masterbuilts!

Excellent choice for beginners: Even if you have no prior experience in BBQ-ing, Electric Smokers won't be that much of a trouble for you, mainly thanks to their streamlined cooking process and ease of use. They are safer and more comfortable to control, which makes it perfect for beginners.

Easy to clean and maintain: Masterbuilt's don't require you to use any messy charcoal or gas as fuel, therefore cleaning Electric Smokers is extremely easy. There isn't much fuel residue left to deal with, and the stainless steel enclosure can be cleaned by simply wiping off the surface.

Why Choose Masterbuilt?

Masterbuilt Smokers have made a name for themselves in recent years for being incredibly efficient, user-friendly and easy going Electric Smokers available in the market! These Smokers are fantastic for newcomers and experienced individuals alike and offer a great way to penetrate the world of Smokers.

But even still, if you are wondering as to "Why" you should choose Masterbuilt over others, here's a quick breakdown:

- **Extremely Cost Efficient:** Despite the excellent design of Masterbuilt Smokers, they are comparatively cheap and easy to buy. Clocking at somewhere between 100-400$, these are the first choice of hundreds of top chefs all around the world.
- **Built To Endure:** Masterbuilt Smokers are carefully designed and built with premium and long lasting materials that allow them to withstand the harshness of long-term Smoking. This makes them perfect companions for the first phase of any young and learning Smoker.
- **Impressive Flavors:** The versatility and flexibility of Masterbuilt Smokers allow a user to fully customize their experience by tinkering with the temperature, smoke formation and woods used. All of these factors play an enormous role in creating the SMOKED flavour possible.

The Top 3 Masterbuilt Smokers To Look For

With the basics covered and out of the way, let me introduce you to the top 3 Masterbuilt Smokers available in the market right now!

With the wide variety of different smokers to choose from, the following three should always be on the top of your list when considering your new Smoker.

Masterbuilt's Smoker With Front Controlling Viewing Window, RF Remove Controlling, 40 Inch

If you are in the market looking for a top-notch Smoker that won't break your budget, the 40 Inch Remote Controlled Masterbuilt Smoker should be your first choice! The Smoker comes with an additional cooling space, external chip feeding chute that allows for both wood and fuel and a sizable internal drip tray.

Additional features of the Smoker include a four-track system, curved backend, accessible and straightforward functionality, making it extremely easy to use, even for beginners!

Rest assured, with this Smoker, you will get the complete "Bang" for your buck, and it will undoubtedly meet and even surpass your expectation.

At the time of writing, it had a price tag of 600$+

THE 30 INCH MASTERBUILT BLACK-COLORED ELECTRIC AND ANALOG SMOKER

The second option that I got here is for those individuals who are looking for more stylistic flair. The 30-inch Analog Electric Smoker by Masterbuilt is a gorgeous Smokehouse unit that does not sacrifice on any functionality. The housing of this particular model takes inspiration from Masterbuilt's intro Smoker models and thus does an excellent job of being both retro and modern.

The controllable thermostat installed in the appliance allows you to control the temperature without much difficulty easily. This is made even more comfortable thanks to the pre-installed thermometer that ensures that your smoke never exceeds your desired temperature.

The unique design of the smoker also allows for a wood chip tray and water pan housed inside the unit.

Unlike many of Masterbuilt's earlier models, this appliance has support for the temperature of 100 degrees F minimum to 400 degrees F maximum! Meaning, you can experiment with a wide variety of meats as you move forward with your Smoking journey.

At the time of writing, it had a price tag of 168$

MASTERBUILT'S 30 INCH DIGITAL AND ELECTRIC SMOKER WITH TOP CONTROLLER

The third model that I picked for you guys is the updated version of the one that I discussed right above! Asides from the already impressive smoking experience offered by the Analog model, this appliance has a few nifty add-ons that make your Smoking experience even more pleasant.

This Smokehouse unit also sports the perfect marriage of style and functionality with improved digital regulators that provide added precision while reading the temperatures.

Experienced Smokers already know that most issues regarding such devices arise from the temperature control mechanism, as slight alterations in the temperature may result in over/undercooking of the food.

Masterbuilt has taken all the precautions to ensure that nothing like that happens with this device as the digital controller included with the model helps to make precise and accurate temperature adjustments that are carefully maintained all throughout the smoking session.

The digital input panel of the device boasts an excellent 24-hour clock feature that automatically turns the Smoker off once the food is cooked.

And as a bonus, the loading cabinet is situated on the outside of the smoker. Therefore you won't have to open the central unit every single time you have to add more chips or refuel the unit! This mostly helps to prevent heat loss and allows for even smoking.

And to top everything off (literally), this particular model has a top regulator that provides a temperature control ranging between 100 to 275 degree F, making this device ideal for low-temperature smoking.

At the time of writing, it had a price tag of 177$

Buying The Right Smoker

Buying and setting up a Smoker environment isn't an easy task, neither is it cheap. Especially for beginners!

These appliances are considerably more expensive than a simple backyard BBQ and require a right amount of dedication to ensure that everything goes smoothly.

To help save you from a heap of trouble moving forward! This brief section will elaborate on which factors you should consider before purchasing your very own Smoker.

Your Budget

Smokers come in a wide variety of shape and sizes that start 500$ and goes all the way up to 10,000$! The best way to make your budget is by considering the factors below and researching the best Smoker suitable for your needs.

Your Space Availability

You should keep in mind that there are two types of Smoker shapes in general. Side Smokers and Vertical Smokers! Side Smokers tend to require a lot more space than Vertical Smokers, so choose the right one depending on how much space you have.

Usage Frequency

If you are planning on using your Smoker occasionally just for the holidays, or once in the blue then going for a simple indoor stovetop smoker would be better. They are relatively inexpensive and user-friendly.

However, if your lifestyle includes a lot of "Big Time" outdoor parties or family gatherings, then investing in a full sized outdoor Smoker would be the better option.

How Much Available Time You Have For Smoking

Keep in mind that Smokers that use wood or charcoal as fuel requires much more care and labour when smoking food as opposed to Electric Smokers such as the Masterbuilt one's that are way easier to use and time-saving.

If you already have a Smoker, awesome! If not, make sure to go through the above factors to ensure that you are buying the best one for the job.

Learning To Use The Masterbuilt Controls

One of the main reason as to "Why" people love the Masterbuilt Smokers so much! Is the fact they are incredibly versatile and easy to use.

That being said, you should keep in mind that they are still no walk in the park! The art of smoking requires an incredible amount of patience and devotion to master the basics.

But let's not worry about that right now! Must we learn to walk before diving into the details right?

Let me first give you a brief intro as to how you can use the digital controls of your Masterbuilt Smoker to set-up various parameters and use the accompanying devices.

Setting Temperature

- Press the "ON" button
- Press "SET TEMP" button after the LED blinks up
- Use the "+/-" buttons to adjust the temperature accordingly
- Press "SET TEMP" again to finalize your selection

Setting Timer

- Press "SET TIME" button after LED for HOUR Links up
- Use the "+/-" buttons to adjust the HOUR accordingly
- Press "SET TIME" Button again to lock the time in the selected parameter. The minute's section of the timer will start blinking next
- Use the "+/-" buttons to adjust the minutes accordingly
- Press "SET TIME" one last time to lock the minutes and you are good to go!

Using Meat Probe

- Insert the meat probe right into the centre/thickest part of the part for best results
- Press and hold "MEAT PROBE" button, which will light up the LED display and reveal the internal temperature of the probed meat
- Once MEAT PROBE button is released, the LED display will go back to either temperature or timer mode

Using Light

- Press the LIGHT button to turn on the light
- Press the LIGHT button again to turn the lights off

Keeping Your Smoker In Top Shape

Try to follow these steps occasionally, Especially if you haven't used your Smoker in a long time. This will set it up for the task at hand.

- Carefully clean the inside of your smoker with mild soap and wipe every inch, rinse everything with water and let it air dry

- Spray the inside with cooking oil and coat all surfaces
- Place empty water pan inside and set your Smoker to Smoke for 3 hours at Max Temp

Some Healthy Tips

The following tips will not only help you in your Masterbuilt Smoker journey but smoke in general!

- Often you may notice that your meat has reached its desired internal temperature way before you are ready to serve it! In situations like these, the best thing to do is wrap the meat in aluminium foil and reduce temperature loss until you are ready to serve and eat it.
- Always make sure never to overload your Smoker! Keep enough room for air circulation as overloading may result in uneven cooking.
- If your recipe asks you to apply BBQ sauce or other wet ingredients, a right way is to add them an hour before the cooking is complete (and wrapping it in foil afterwards). This helps the meat to absorb the flavour even more.
- On the other hand, you can always use Dry Rubs before placing the meat in your Smoker
- Make sure never to cover the racks with aluminium foil as they will prevent the heat from circulating inside

Smoke and Meat

TYPES OF SMOKERS

ELECTRIC SMOKERS

The electric smoker is the best smoker because it is very simple to use. Just set it, put your food in it and leave the rest of the work to the smoker. There is nothing an electric smoker can't grill, be it seafood, poultry, meat, cheese or bread. It requires little attention unlike other smokers like filling water bin, lighting wood or charcoal and checking on fuel frequently. Yes, unlike traditional smoker, electric smoker just need 2 to 4 ounce of wood chips that turns out a delicious and flavorful smoky food. Furthermore, they maintain cooking temperature really well. On the other hand, it sleek and stylish look and small size make it appropriate if you are living in an apartment or condo. Due to their simpler functions and hassle-free cooking, the electric smoker is a good choice for beginner cooks who want to get started with smoking food.

GAS SMOKERS

Gas smokers or propane smoker are much like a gas grill using propane as a fuel. Therefore, the heat for cooking remains consistent and steady. Furthermore, gas smokers are as easy to use, just set the temperature and walk away. However, frequent checks need to be done to make sure fuel doesn't run out. It isn't a big issue but one should keep in mind. And the best part, a gas smoker can be used when there is no electricity or when you need an oven. A gas smoker can take up to cooking temperature to 450 degrees, making this smoker flexible to be used as an oven. Another fantastic feature of gas smoker is its portability so they can use anywhere. Just pack it and take it along with you on your camping trips or other outdoor adventures.

CHARCOAL SMOKERS

Nothing can beat the flavor charcoal gives to your food. Its best flavor just simply can't match with any other smoker flavor. Unfortunately, setting a charcoal smoker, tuning fuel, maintaining cooking temperature and checking food can be a pain and you might burn the food. Not to worry, these hassles of a charcoal smoker does go away with practice and experience. Therefore, a charcoal smoker suits perfectly for serious grillers and barbecue purist who want flavors.

PALLET SMOKERS

Pellet smokers are making a surge due to their best feature of a pallet of maintaining a consistent temperature. It contains an automated system to drop pallets which frees the cook to monitor fuel level. The addition of thermostat gives the user the complete control the cooking temperature and grilling of food under ideal condition. In addition, the smoking food uses the heat from hardwood which gives food a delicious flavor. The only downside of pallet smoker is their high cost between the ranges of $100 to %600.

TYPES OF SMOKER WOODS

Smoker wood is an important element which you need to decide correctly to cook a delicious smoked food. The reason is that smoker chips of woods impart different flavors on the food you are cooking in the smoker. Therefore, you should know which smoker wood should be used to create a delicious smoked food. Here is the lowdown of smoker woods and which food is best with them.

1. Alder: A lighter smoker wood with natural sweetness.
   Best to smoke: Any fish especially salmon, poultry and game birds.
2. Maple: This smoker wood has a mild and sweet flavor. In addition, its sweet smoke gives the food a dark appearance. For better flavor, use it as a combination with alder, apple or oak smoker woods.
   Best to smoke: Vegetables, cheese, and poultry.
3. Apple: A mild fruity flavor smoker wood with natural sweetness. When mixed with oak smoker wood, it gives a great flavor to food. Let food smoke for several hours as the smoke takes a while to permeate the food with the flavors.
   Best to smoke: Poultry, beef, pork, lamb, and seafood.
4. Cherry: This smoker wood is an all-purpose fruity flavor wood for any type of meat. Its smoke gives the food a rich, mahogany color. Try smoking by mixing it with alder, oak, pecan and hickory smoker wood.
   Best to smoke: Chicken, turkey, ham, pork, and beef.
5. Oak: Oakwood gives a medium flavor to food which is stronger compared to apple wood and cherry wood and lighter compared to hickory. This versatile smoker wood works well blended with hickory, apple, and cherry woods.
   Best to smoke: Sausages, brisket, and lamb.
6. Peach and Pear: Both smoker woods are similar to each other. They give food a subtle light and fruity flavor with the addition of natural sweetness.
   Best to smoke: Poultry, pork and game birds.
7. Hickory: Hickory wood infuses a strong sweet and bacon flavor into the food, especially meat cuts. Don't over smoke with this wood as it can turn the taste of food bitter.
   Best to smoke: Red meat, poultry, pork shoulder, ribs.
8. Pecan: This sweet smoker wood lends the food a rich and nutty flavor. Use it with Mesquite wood to balance its sweetness.
   Best to smoke: Poultry, pork.
9. Walnut: This strong flavored smoker wood is often used as a mixing wood due to its slightly bitter flavor. Use walnut wood with lighter smoke woods like pecan wood or apple wood.
   Best to smoke: Red meat and game birds.
10. Grape: Grape wood chips give a sweet berry flavor to food. It's best to use these wood chips with apple wood chips.
    Best to smoke: Poultry
11. Mulberry: Mulberry wood chips is similar to apple wood chips. It adds natural sweetness and gives berry finish to the food.
    Best to smoke: Ham and Chicken.

12- Mesquite: Mesquite wood chips flavor is earthy and slightly harsh and bitter. It burns fast and strongly hot. Therefore, don't use it for longer grilling.

Best to smoke: Red meat, dark meat.

THE DIFFERENT TYPES OF CHARCOAL AND THEIR BENEFITS

Charcoal is one of the efficient fuels for smoking. It burns hot, with more concentrated fire. Smoking food with charcoal is awesome. Though lighting charcoals, regulating airflows and controlling the heat is always a challenge, however, the excellent taste of food is worth this challenge. But, keep in mind that not all charcoals are equal and selecting one is a matter of preference.

LUMP CHARCOAL:

Lump charcoal or hardwood is the first choice of griller as a better fuel source. It is basically made by burning wood logs in an underground pit for a few days. As a result, water, sap, and other substances in log burn out, leaving behind a pure char or lump charcoal. This charcoal burns pure, hot and efficiently. They burn hotter in the beginner and burn cooler by the end. Therefore, lump charcoal is a good choice for broiling quickly or searing food at intense heat. In addition, the lump char also add the aroma of wood smoke into the food which takes the taste to another level of gastronomical heaven. Since, lump charcoal cool its fire in 30 minutes, replenish fire to maintain the temperature which takes only 5 to 10 minutes by adding few unlit coals. It's recommended to use lump charcoal with a combination of wood chips like maple, oak or hickory and refuel this wood chips every 40 minutes during smoking food.

CHARCOAL BRIQUETTES:

Charcoal briquettes are actually crushed charcoal. The major benefit of using this natural charcoal is its even shape and size. This is done by adding chemical binders and fillers like coal dust and compressing into a pillow shape. Therefore, creating a bed of coals is very easy with charcoal briquettes which are quite hard with uneven and irregular charcoals. The only downside is that they burn very quickly, more than lump charcoal. This creates a short window for smoking food, therefore, more briquettes need to add during grilling.

THE DIFFERENCE BETWEEN BARBECUING A MEAT AND SMOKING IT?

There are two main ways to cook meat that has become an increasingly popular cooking method: smoking or barbecuing. They are both different and require different cooking equipment, temperature, and timing. Following is the full comparison between smoking and barbecue.

BARBECUING MEAT:

Barbecue is a slow cooking, indirectly over low heat between 200 to 250 degrees F. Therefore, it is best suited for beef brisket, whole pig, turkeys or pork shoulder. These animals tend to have tough muscles which need slow cooking over low heat to get a moist and tender meat. It turns out an extremely tender and flavorful meat. The best example of a perfect barbecue is falling of meat off the bones. During the barbecue, the fuel needs to be filled frequently but do this quickly, as lifting lid of burner exposes meat to air which can turn it dry.

For barbecuing meat, the grill needs to be preheated until hot. For this light enough charcoals or bкisquettes so that their fire turns down for cooking. In the meantime, season meat and then when grill reaches to perfect cooking temperature, place seasoned meat on it. Having grill on perfect temperature is essential as meat won't stick to grilling grate.

Equipment: Fire pit, grill or a charcoal burner with lid.

Fueling: Lump wood charcoal, charcoal briquettes or wood chips combination like apple. Cherry and oak wood chips.

Best to smoke: A big cut of meats like Briskets, whole chicken, sausages, jerky, pork, and ribs.

Temperature: 190 to 300 degrees F

Timing: 2 hours to a day long.

SMOKING MEAT:

Smoking is one of the oldest cooking technique dating back to the first people living in caves. It was traditionally a food preservation method and with the time, its popularity never died. Smoking is a related process of barbecue. It's the best cooking method to bring out the rich and deep flavor of meat that tastes heavenly when meat is smoked until it comes off the bone.

During smoking, food is cooked below 200 degrees F cooking temperature. Therefore, smoking food requires a lot of time and patience. It infuses woody flavor into the meat and turns a silky and fall-of-bone meat. There are three ways to smoke food, cold smoke, hot smoke and adding liquid smoke. In these three types of smoking methods, liquid smoke is becoming increasingly common. Its main advantage is that smoke flavor is controlled. In addition, the effect of liquid smoke on meat is immediate.

There is another smoking method which called water smoking. It uses water smoker which is specifically designed to incorporate water in the smoking process. The water helps in controlling the temperature of smoker which is great for large cut meats for long hours.

Equipment: A closed container or high-tech smoker.

Fueling: The container will need an external source for a smoke. Wood chips are burn to add smoky flavor to the meat. However, the frequent check should be made to monitor and adjust temperature for smoking.

Best to smoke: A big cut of meats like Briskets, whole chicken, pork, and ribs.

Temperature: 68 to 176 degrees F

Timing: 1 hour to 2 weeks

THE CORE DIFFERENCE BETWEEN COLD AND HOT SMOKING

There are two ways to smoke meat that is cold smoking and hot smoking. In cold smoking, meat is cooked between 68 to 86 degrees F until smoked but moist. It is a good choice to smoke meat like chicken breast, steak, beef, pork chops, salmon, and cheese. The cold smoking concern with adding flavor to the meat rather than cooking. Therefore, when the meat is cold smoked, it should be cured, baked or steamed before serving.

On the other hand, hot smoking cooks the meat completely, in addition, to enhance its flavor. Therefore, meat should be a cook until its internal temperature is between 126 to 176 degrees F. Don't let meat temperature reach 185 degrees F as at this temperature, meat shrinks or buckles. Large meat cuts like brisket, ham, ribs and pulled pork turns out great when hot smoked.

THE CORE ELEMENTS OF SMOKING

There are six essential elements of smoking.

1- Wood chips: Chip of woods are used as a fuel either alone or in combination with charcoals. In addition, these chips add fantastic flavor to the meat. Therefore, chips of wood should only be used which suits best to the meat.
2- Smoker: There are basically four choices from which a smoker should be the pick. The choices are an electric smoker, charcoal smoker, gas smoker and pellet smoker. Each has its own advantages and downsides.
3- Smoking time: Smoking time is essential for perfect of meat cuts. It is actually the time when the internal temperature reaches its desired values. It may take 2 hours up to more than two weeks.
4- Meat: The star of the show is meat that needs to be more tender, juicy and flavorful after smoking. Make sure, the meat you sure has fat trimmed from it. In addition, it should complement the wood of chips.
5- Rub: Rubs, mixture or salt and spices, add sweetness and heat to the meat. They should be prepared in such a way that all types of flavor should be balanced in the meat.
6- Mops: Mops or liquid is often used during smoking meat. It adds a little bit flavor to the meat and maintains tenderness and moisture throughout the smoking process.

THE BASIC PREPARATIONS FOR SMOKING MEAT

CHOOSING SMOKER

The major and foremost step is to choose a smoker. You can invest in any type of the smoker: charcoal smoker, gas smoker or an electric smoker. A charcoal smoker runs for a long time and maintain steadier heat in the smoker and give meat pure flavors. A good choice for beginner cook for smoking meat is a gas smoker where there is no need to monitor temperature but it comes with a downside that meat won't have much flavor compared to charcoal. On the other hand, the simplest, easiest and popular smoker is an electric smoker. Cooking with electric smoker involves only two-step: turn it on, put meat in it and walk away. Read more details about smokers in the section "type of smokers".

CHOOSING FUEL

Wood chips add a unique flavor to the meat, therefore, select that wood chips that would enhance the taste of meat. Some wood of chips have a stronger flavor, some have mild while others are just enough to be alone for smoking. Check out the section titled "types of smoker wood" to get to know and decide chips of wood that will complement your meat.

TYPE OF SMOKING METHOD

You have two choices to smoke meat, either using wet smoking, dry smoking, liquid smoke or water smoking. Read the section "The core difference between cold and hot smoking" to find out differences between each. In addition, go through smoking meat portion in the section "the difference between barbecuing a meat and smoking it".

SOAKING CHIPS OF WOOD

Wood chips need to soak in order to last longer for fueling smoking. The reason is dry wood that burns quickly and this means, adding fuel to the smoker which can result in dry smoked meat. There isn't any need of using wood chips when smoking for a shorter time. Prepare wood chips by soaking them in water for at least 4 hours before starting smoking. Then drain chips and wrap and seal them in an aluminium foil. Use toothpick or fork for poking holes into the wood chips bag.

SET SMOKER

Each type of smoker have its own way to start smoking. For wood or charcoal smoker, first, light up half of the charcoals and wait until their flame goes down. Then add remaining charcoal and wood chips if using. Wait they are lighted and giving heat completely, then push charcoal aside and place meat on the other side of grilling grate.

This is done to make sure that meat is indirectly smoked over low heat. Continue adding charcoal and/or soaked wood chips into the smoker.

For gas/propane or electric smoker, just turn it on according to manufacturer guideline and then add soaked wood chips into chip holder and fill water receptacle if a smoker has one. Either make use of the incorporated thermostat or buy your own to monitor the internal temperature of the smoker. When smoker reaches to desired preheated temperature, add meat to it.

SELECTING MEAT FOR SMOKING

Choose the type of meat which tastes good with a smoky flavor. Following meat goes well for smoking.

Beef: ribs, brisket and corned beef.

Pork: spare ribs, roast, shoulder, and ham.

Poultry: whole chicken, whole turkey, and big game hens.

Seafood: Salmon, scallops, trout, and lobster.

GETTING MEAT READY

Prepare meat according to the recipe. Sometimes meat is cured, marinated or simply seasoned with the rub. These preparation methods ensure smoked meat turn out flavorful, tender and extremely juicy.

Brine is a solution to treating poultry, pork or ham. It involves dissolving brine ingredients in water poured into a huge container and then adding meat to it. Then let soak for at least 8 hours and after that, rinse it well and pat dry before you begin smoking.

Marinate treat beef or briskets and add flavors to it. It's better to make deep cuts in meat to let marinate ingredients deep into it. Drain meat or smoke it straightaway.

Rubs are commonly used to treat beef, poultry or ribs. They are actually a combination of salt and many spices, rubbed generously all over the meat. Then the meat is left to rest for at least 2 hours or more before smoking it.

Before smoking meat, make sure it is at room temperature. This ensures meat is cooked evenly and reach its internal temperature at the end of smoking time.

PLACING MEAT INTO THE SMOKER

Don't place the meat directly over heat into the smoker because the main purpose of smoking is cooking meat at low temperature. Set aside your fuel on one side of the smoker and place meat on the other side and let cook.

Smoking time: The smoking time of meat depends on the internal temperature. For this, use a meat thermometer and insert it into the thickest part of the meat. The smoking time also varies with the size of meat. Check recipes to determine the exact smoking time for the meat.

BASTING MEAT

Some recipes call for brushing meat with thin solutions, sauces or marinade. This step not only makes meat better in taste, it also helps to maintain moisture in meat through the smoking process. Read recipe to check out if basting is necessary.

Taking out meat: When the meat reaches its desired internal temperature, remove it from the smoker. Generally, poultry should be removed from smoker when its internal temperature reaches to 165 degrees F. For ground meats, ham, and pork, the internal temperature should be 160 degrees F. 145 degrees F is the internal temperature for chops, roast, and steaks.

CONCLUSION

As you can see from these recipes, the world of smoking is only as limited as your imagination! Sweet, savory, vegetable, mineral, meat- you can smoke almost anything. As you get more comfortable with these recipes, feel free to start experimenting on your own. The basic principles hold true, but your own taste buds can drive you. Good luck, and happy smoking!

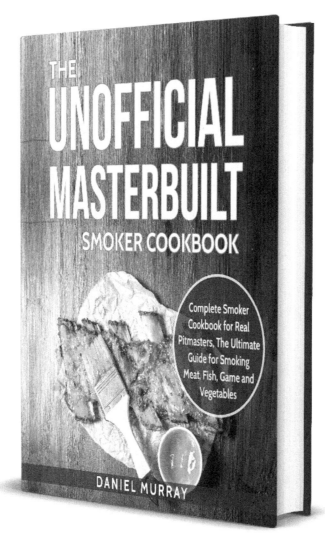

GET YOUR FREE GIFT

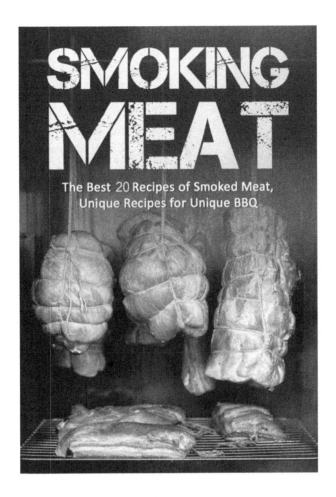

Subscribe to our Mail List and get your FREE copy of the book

'Smoking Meat: The Best 20 Recipes of Smoked Meat, Unique Recipes for Unique BBQ'

https://tiny.cc/smoke20

OTHER BOOKS BY DANIEL MURRAY

https://www.amazon.com/dp/B07D8NFZ3F

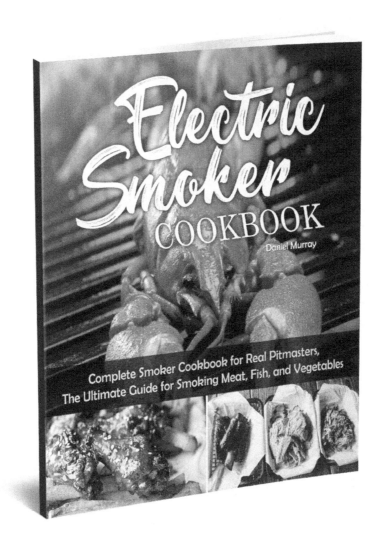

HTTPS://WWW.AMAZON.COM/DP/B07DKZ3NSK

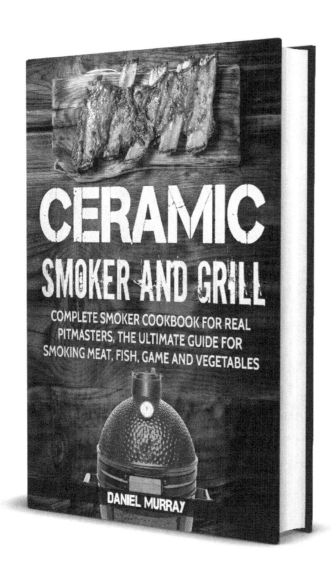

HTTPS://WWW.AMAZON.COM/DP/B07GSKRLB8

© *Copyright 2018 – Daniel Murray - All rights reserved.*

In no way is it legal to reproduce, duplicate, or transmit any part of this document in either electronic means or in printed format. Recording of this publication is strictly prohibited and any storage of this document is not allowed unless with written permission from the publisher. All rights reserved.

ISBN: 9781728684321

The information provided herein is stated to be truthful and consistent, in that any liability, in terms of inattention or otherwise, by any usage or abuse of any policies, processes, or directions contained within is the solitary and utter responsibility of the recipient reader. Under no circumstances will any legal responsibility or blame be held against the publisher for any reparation, damages, or monetary loss due to the information herein, either directly or indirectly.

Respective authors own all copyrights not held by the publisher.

Legal Notice:

This book is copyright protected. This is only for personal use. You cannot amend, distribute, sell, use, quote or paraphrase any part or the content within this book without the consent of the author or copyright owner. Legal action will be pursued if this is breached.

Disclaimer Notice:

Please note the information contained within this document is for educational and entertainment purposes only. Every attempt has been made to provide accurate, up to date and reliable complete information. No warranties of any kind are expressed or implied. Readers acknowledge that the author is not engaging in the rendering of legal, financial, medical or professional advice.

By reading this document, the reader agrees that under no circumstances are we responsible for any losses, direct or indirect, which are incurred as a result of the use of information contained within this document, including, but not limited to, —errors, omissions, or inaccuracies.

Made in the USA
Columbia, SC
16 April 2019